Cultural Holidays

Christmas

by L. L. Owens
illustrated by Holli Conger

Content Consultant: Dr. Pamela R. Frese
Professor of Anthropology, College of Wooster

visit us at www.abdopublishing.com

Published by Magic Wagon, a division of the ABDO Group, 8000 West 78th Street, Edina, Minnesota 55439.

Printed in the United States.

Text by L. L. Owens
Illustrations by Holli Conger
Edited by Mari Kesselring
Interior layout and design by Becky Daum
Cover design by Becky Daum
Special thanks to cultural consultant Dr. James F. McGrath, Associate Professor of Religion, Butler University

Library of Congress Cataloging-in-Publication Data

Owens, L. L.
Christmas / by L.L. Owens ; illustrated by Holli Conger ; content consultant, Pamela R. Frese.
p. cm. — (Cultural holidays)
Includes index.
ISBN 978-1-60270-601-9
1. Christmas—Juvenile literature. I. Frese, Pamela R. II. Conger, Holli, ill. III. Title.
GT4985.5.O9 2010
394.2663—dc22

2008050553

Table of Contents

What Is Christmas?

On December 25, people all over the world celebrate Christmas. It is a special day. People gather with family, sing carols, and give gifts. For Christians, Christmas honors the birth of Jesus Christ.

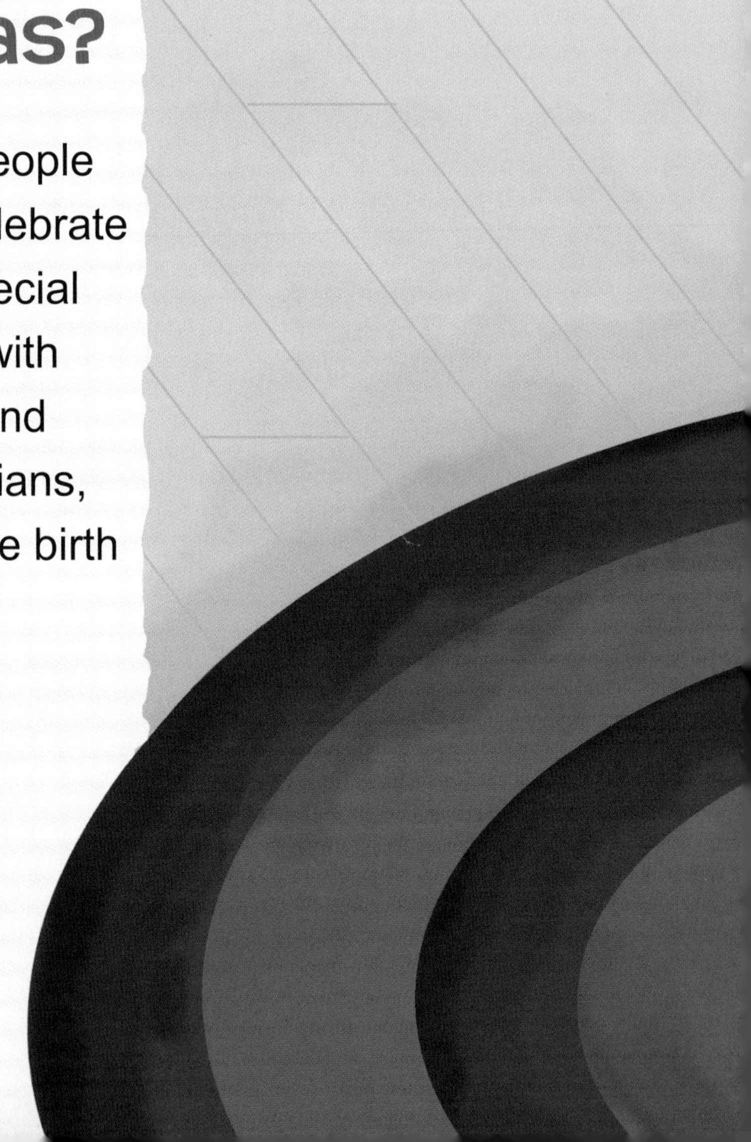

The Christmas Story

The Bible is the Christian holy book. It has stories about Jesus's birth. Jesus was born more than 2,000 years ago. His mother was Mary. An angel told Mary that she would have a baby. The angel said that her child would be God's son.

Mary and her husband, Joseph, went to Bethlehem. On a clear night, Jesus was born. There was no room at the inn. So he was born in a stable.

Nearby a group of shepherds were watching their sheep in the fields. A crowd of angels appeared. They told the shepherds to visit Jesus. The shepherds went to see the baby. When they saw Jesus, they knew he was special.

Three wise men from the East also came to see Jesus. A bright star showed them the way. The wise men gave Jesus gifts.

The wise men gave Jesus gifts of gold, frankincense, and myrrh.

We do not know the exact date of Jesus's birth. It was so long ago. We do know that the Romans celebrated Christmas on December 25 in the early fourth century. The holiday spread from there.

Rituals and Customs

Christians have special customs on Christmas. Many people go to church on Christmas Eve or Christmas Day. At church people say prayers. Sometimes they listen to the story of Jesus's birth.

Some churches have Christmas pageants. In a Christmas pageant, children act out the story of Jesus's birth or another Christmas story.

Dear Santa,

For many people, Christmas is not only a religious holiday. Many people enjoy non-religious Christmas activities. Here are some ways to celebrate Christmas:

- Give gifts
- Send greeting cards
- Sing carols
- Wait for Santa Claus
- Decorate a tree
- String lights outside
- Bake cookies and other treats
- Eat a special holiday dinner

Decorations, Foods, and Carols

People decorate their homes for Christmas in many ways. People might hang up holly and mistletoe. Those who stand under mistletoe are supposed to kiss each other!

Most families put up Christmas trees in their homes. They put lights and ornaments on the trees. This is called "trimming the tree." Many people put a star on the tops of their trees.

Christmas trees come in all shapes and sizes. New York City puts up a huge Christmas tree in Rockefeller Center every year in time for Christmas. In India people decorate mango and banana trees for Christmas.

People eat many foods on Christmas. For Christmas dinner, they might eat turkey, ham, roast beef, fish, or goose.

People often bake Christmas cookies. Some Christmas cookies are made in special shapes. The shapes are Christmas symbols such as stars, trees, and angels.

On Christmas Eve in Denmark, people serve rice pudding with an almond hidden inside. If you find the nut, your next year will be lucky.

People love Christmas carols! “Joy to the World,” “Jingle Bells,” and “Santa Claus Is Coming to Town” are some favorites. Some people go caroling on Christmas.

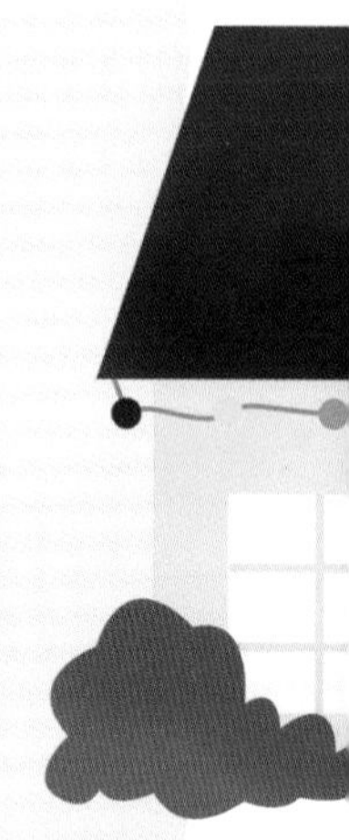

Caroling has been around for a long time. It dates back to the Middle Ages in England. Poor people would sing outside houses. People in the houses would give the carolers food or money if they liked the song.

Celebrations Today

On Christmas Day, many people visit with friends and family. They often have a meal together. They might give gifts. People like to spend Christmas with those they love.

A big part of Christmas for many people is gift giving. Gifts are usually opened on Christmas Day or Christmas Eve. For Christians, giving gifts reminds them of the wise men giving gifts to Jesus.

On Christmas morning in the United States, children wake up to gifts brought by Santa Claus. Many believe Santa leaves the North Pole in his sleigh on Christmas Eve. He works hard all night to bring gifts to children.

Children leave stockings out before they go to bed. Santa fills the stockings with candy. He also leaves gifts for the children under the tree. Maybe the children of the house have left milk and cookies for him!

Santa has nine reindeer that pull his sleigh. Their names are Dasher, Dancer, Prancer, Vixen, Comet, Cupid, Donner, Blitzen, and Rudolph.

Christmas is celebrated all around the world. But it is different everywhere. For people living in Iran, Christmas is known as "Little Feast." Each child gets new clothes to wear for the holiday.

Instead of Santa, some countries have other Christmas visitors. In France, children fill their shoes with hay and carrots for *Père Noël*. He lets his donkey eat the treats. He leaves gifts for the good children.

No matter where you are, Christmas can be a fun holiday. Will you celebrate Christmas this year?

Christmas Carol

"We Wish You a Merry Christmas" is a fun carol to sing with your friends and family.

We Wish You a Merry Christmas

We wish you a merry Christmas;
We wish you a merry Christmas;
We wish you a merry Christmas and a happy New Year.
Good tidings we bring to you and your kin;
Good tidings for Christmas and a happy New Year.

Oh, bring us some figgy pudding;
Oh, bring us some figgy pudding;
Oh, bring us some figgy pudding and a cup of good cheer.

We won't go until we get some;
We won't go until we get some;
We won't go until we get some, so bring some out here.
We wish you a merry Christmas and a happy New Year.

Glossary

angel—a spiritual being.

carol—a song of joy.

Christian—a person who believes in Jesus Christ.

holy—belonging to God.

religious—relating to a religion.

shepherd—a person who takes care of sheep.

On the Web

To learn more about Christmas, visit ABDO Group online at **www.abdopublishing.com**. Web sites about Christmas are featured on our Book Links page. These links are routinely monitored and updated to provide the most current information available.

Index